THE OXFORD BOOK OF

Christmas
Organ Music

Book 2

Compiled by
Robert Gower

OXFORD
UNIVERSITY PRESS

OXFORD
UNIVERSITY PRESS

Great Clarendon Street, Oxford OX2 6DP,
United Kingdom

Oxford University Press is a department of the University of Oxford.
It furthers the University's objective of excellence in research, scholarship,
and education by publishing worldwide. Oxford is a registered trade mark of
Oxford University Press in the UK and in certain other countries

First published 2024

ISBN 978-0-19-356063-5

Music and text origination by Andrew Jones
Printed in Great Britain on acid-free paper by
Caligraving Ltd, Thetford, Norfolk.

CONTENTS

PREFACE

In the quest for durability of publication, the compiler of an anthology needs to put aside personal taste, aiming for broad, comprehensive content balance. Period, form, style and length of composition, composer nationality, and degree of technical challenge, together with decisions on new commissions, all demand consideration. Global thinking has advanced since publication of the original *Oxford Book of Christmas Organ Music* in 1995. That collection, consistently in demand, has informed preparation of this second volume. The intervening thirty years have witnessed developments in scholarship, while wider societal attitudes now rightly place greater emphasis on inclusivity, reflected in this anthology through greater diversity.

The working partnership between compiler and editor aims to ensure that the publication contains measured musical variety, providing opportunity for organists to make reacquaintance with some familiar repertoire (albeit in fresh guises) alongside the stimulus provided by new writing. I hope that my excitement in playing music written for this book by Kristina Arakelyan, David Bednall, Iain Farrington, Howard Skempton, and Amy Summers, together with personal discoveries of other contemporary writers (Mark Blatchly, Guy Bovet, Richard Elliott, Alfred Fedak, Benjamin Lamb, and Philip Moore), will be widely shared. I pay tribute to the industry and musicianship of Jonathan Cunliffe (Commissioning and Development Editor at OUP), whose critical oversight allied to patient scrutiny has been integral in seeking to bring attractiveness and balance to a finished publication of highest quality.

Researching over a period of two decades has made significant demands: I am grateful to those who have given assistance, acknowledging in particular, my wife, Pauline, and Frances Pond, now retired Librarian of the Royal College of Organists, without whose long-suffering understanding and cooperation this anthology could not have appeared.

Robert Gower
Auchterhouse, Angus
August 2023

Prelude on 'Carol of the Bells'

(Ukrainian New Year song 'Shchedryk')

KRISTINA ARAKELYAN
(b. 1994)

Based on the traditional Ukrainian New Year song 'Shchedryk', composed by Mykola Leontovych, to which the English text 'Carol of the Bells' was subsequently added by Peter Wilhousky.

Noël

ADOLPHE ADAM
(1803–56)
arr. Arthur Boyse and Robert Gower

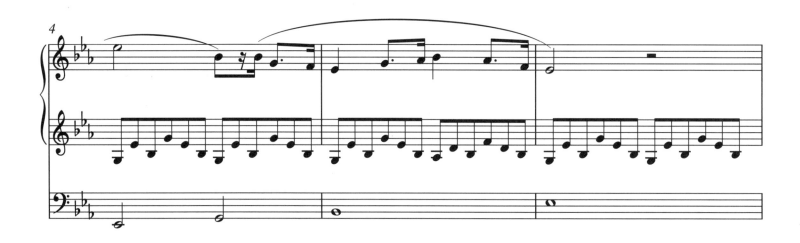

Sleigh Ride

LEROY ANDERSON
(1908–75)
arr. Thomas Trotter

* Original time signature: 2/2

Lullay, thou little tiny child

CECIL ARMSTRONG GIBBS
(1889–1960)
ed. Robert Gower

Sw.: soft 8'
Gt.: Flute 8', Sw. to Gt.
Ped.: 16', Sw. to Ped.

Sortie on 'Mendelssohn'

('Hark! the herald angels sing')

DAVID BEDNALL
(b. 1979)

Chorale Prelude on 'Der Tag, der ist so freudenreich'

('O hail this brightest day of days')

J. S. BACH
(1685–1750)
BWV 605

Hear, King of Angels

from *Christmas Oratorio*, BWV 248

J. S. BACH
(1685–1750)
arr. Robert Gower

Variations on 'Il était une bergère'

('There was a shepherdess')

MARK BLATCHLY
(b. 1960)

II. Chords (♩s short; ♪s long) (♩ = 76–100)

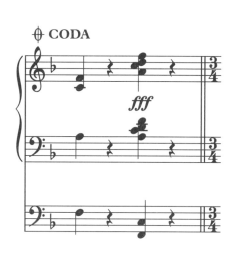

III. Five Valleys (♩ = 108) **Slow, with freedom**

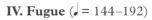

IV. Fugue (♩ = 144–192)

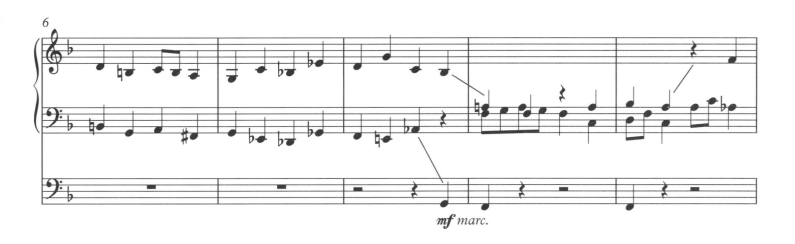

Ave Maria

JOHANNES BRAHMS
(1833–97)
Op. 12
arr. Robert Gower

Separate manuals with balanced registration should be used.

Prelude on 'Stille Nacht, heilige Nacht'

('Silent night! Holy night!')

from *Voici Noël*, Op. 1 No. 6

GUY BOVET
(b. 1942)

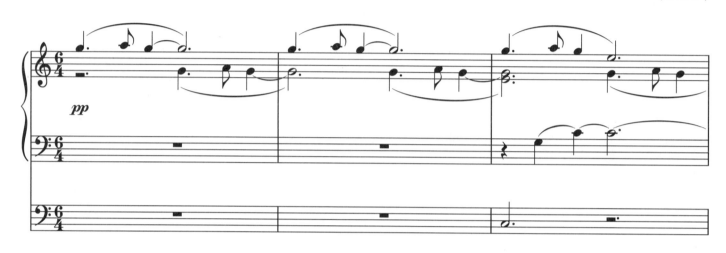

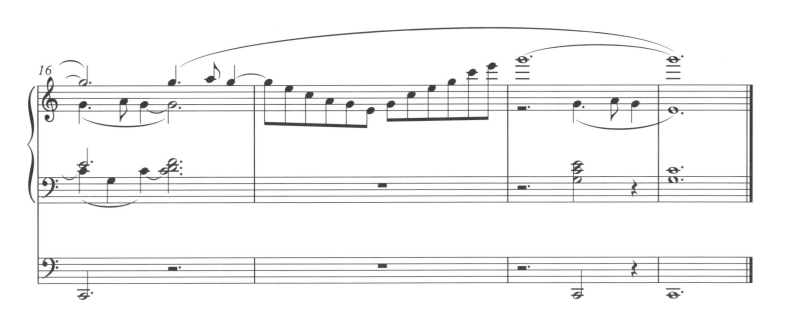

Prelude on 'In dulci jubilo'

No. 1 from *Two Christmas Preludes*, Op. 35

PERCY C. BUCK
(1871–1947)
arr. Robert Gower

Sw.: Voix celeste, super octave ad lib.
Gt.: Flute 8'
Ped.: soft 16', Sw. to Ped.

Chorale Prelude on 'Gottes Sohn ist kommen'

HEINRICH BUTTSTEDT
(1666–1727)

Chorale Prelude on 'Nun komm der Heiden Heiland'

('Now come, Saviour of the heathens')

DIETERICH BUXTEHUDE
(1637–1707)

Auprès de la crèche

HEDWIGE CHRÉTIEN
(1859–1944)
arr. Robert Gower

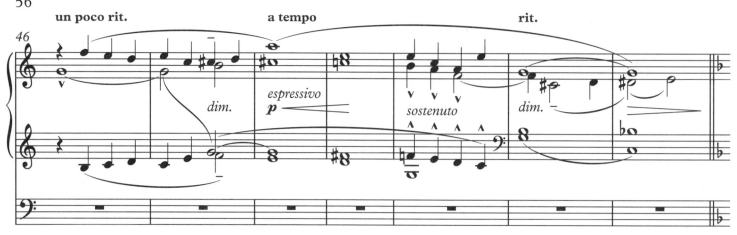

Berceuse de l'Enfant Jésus

HEDWIGE CHRÉTIEN
(1859–1944)
arr. Robert Gower

Puer nobis nascitur

('Unto us is born a son')

JEAN-FRANÇOIS DANDRIEU
(1682–1738)

Grand Jeu

Dialogue

Prélude sur l'Introït de l'Épiphanie

MAURICE DURUFLÉ
(1902–86)

Pos.: Trompette 8'
Réc.: Principal 8', Prestant 4', Doublette 2', Fourniture
Péd.: Soubasse 16', Flûtes 8', 4'

Allegretto (♩ = 108) **La croche égale toujours la croche**

Prelude on 'Gabriel's Message'

('The angel Gabriel from heaven came')

IAIN FARRINGTON
(b. 1977)

Based on the traditional Basque carol.

Toccatina on 'Angels we have heard on high'

RICHARD ELLIOTT
(b. 1957)

Sw.: Foundations 8', 4', Mixture
Gt.: Foundations 8', 4', 2', Mixture, Sw. to Gt.
Ped.: Foundations 16', 8', Sw. to Ped.

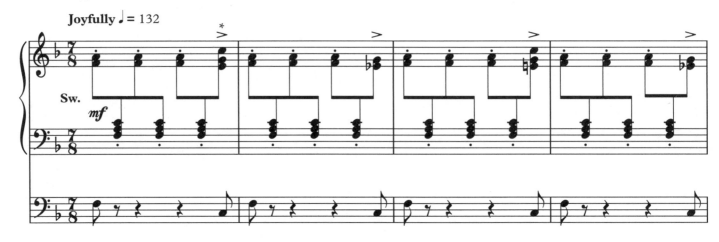

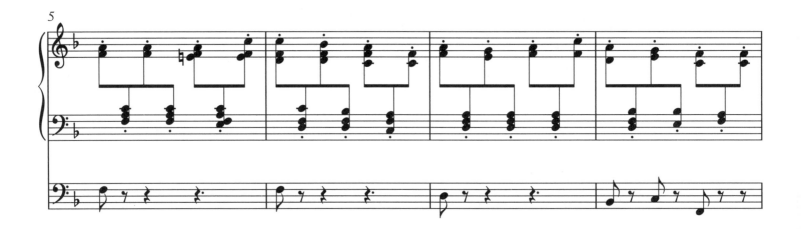

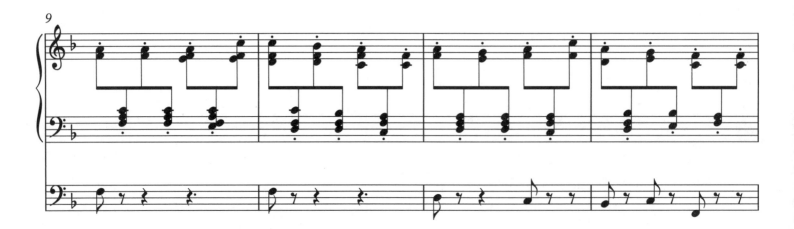

* Optional: in bb. 1–4 and 25–30, accented chords may be played by jumping the right hand to the Great manual.

Based on the traditional French carol 'Les Anges dans nos campagnes'.

Impression on 'We Three Kings'

ALFRED V. FEDAK
(b. 1953)

Sw.: Flute 8', String 8'
Gt.: Flutes 8' and 2⅔'
Ped.: soft Flute 16'

Carol Symphony

(Extract from third movement)

VICTOR HELY-HUTCHINSON
(1901–47)
arr. Robert Gower

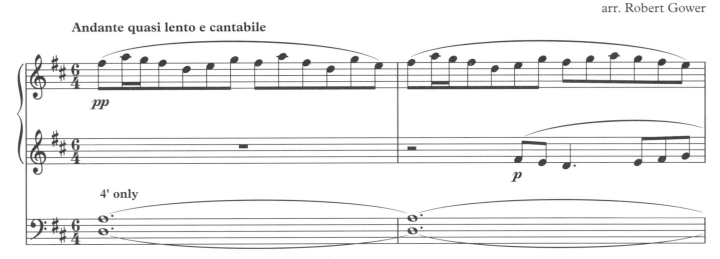

If desired, couple a manual 4' to the pedal for the opening and use the same stop for the RH, playing an octave lower. Registration should be musically graded; the composer's orchestral dynamic markings are shown here.

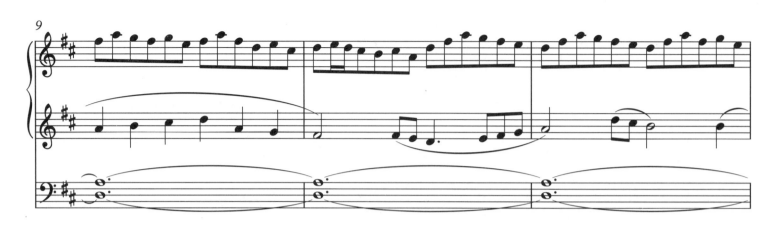

dim. al fine

rit. al fine

ppp

Passacaglia and Chorale on 'The Truth from Above'

('This is the truth sent from above')

BENJAMIN LAMB
(b. 1974)

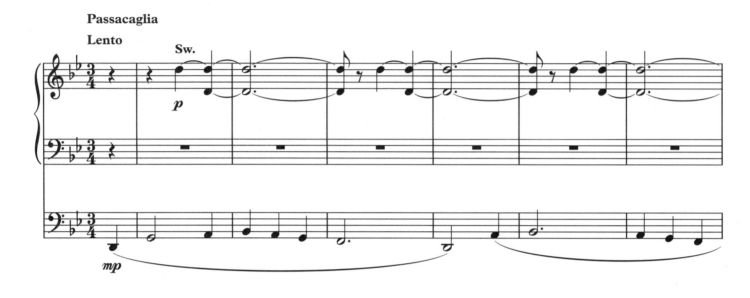

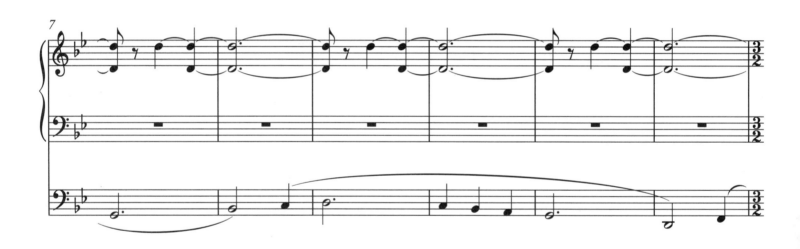

sempre più mosso

* If used before a service, the piece may finish here, allowing a soloist to sing verse 1 of the carol unaccompanied.

Chorale Prelude on
'Wachet auf, ruft uns die Stimme'

('Wake, O wake! with tidings thrilling')

GOTTFRIED AUGUST HOMILIUS
(1714–85)

Chorale Prelude on 'O Jesulein süss, O Jesulein mild'

('O Little One sweet, O Little One mild')

MICHAEL GOTTHARDT FISCHER
(1773–1829)

Sw.: Diapason 8' or soft stops
[or Ch. (or Sw.) Flutes 8', 4']
Ped.: soft 16', (8'), Sw. (or Ch.) to Ped.

rall.

to Rebecca te Velde

Prelude on 'Helmsley'

('Lo! He comes with clouds descending')

LESTER GROOM
(1929–2000)

Sw.: Reed or Cornet 8'
Gt.: Lighter Principals or Flutes 8', 4'
Ped.: 16', 8', Gt. to Ped.

A Fugal Flourish on 'Personent Hodie'

('Long ago, prophets knew')

PHILIP MOORE
(b. 1943)

Sw: 8', 4', 2'
Gt: 8', 4', 2', Mixture
Ch: 8', 4', 2'
Ped: 16', 8', 4', Gt. to Ped.

marcato

marcato

molto rall.

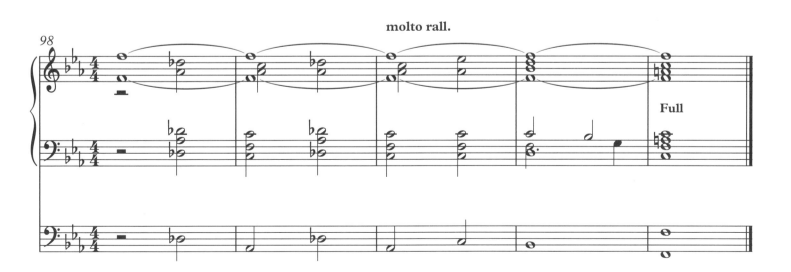

An Old Christmas Carol

('God rest you merry, gentlemen')

ELIZABETH MOUNSEY
(1819–1905)
ed. Robert Gower

Andantino cantabile ♩ = 96

Variation 1
Con moto ♩ = 104

Variation 2

Allegro con spirito ♩ = 112

Variation 3
Allegro vivace agitato ♩= 72

Variation 4

Moderato risoluto ♩ = 104

Variation 5 has been omitted from this publication.

Variation 6

Prestissimo e capricciosa ♩ = 120

Variation 7
Andante tranquillo ♩ = 84

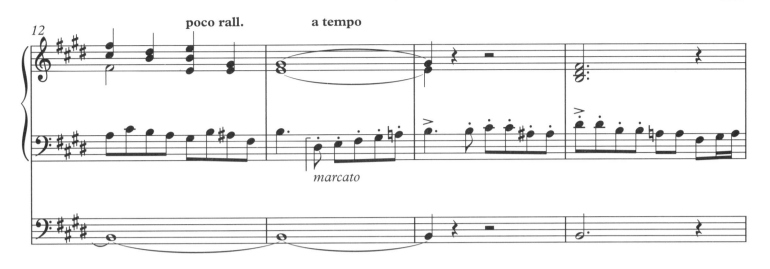

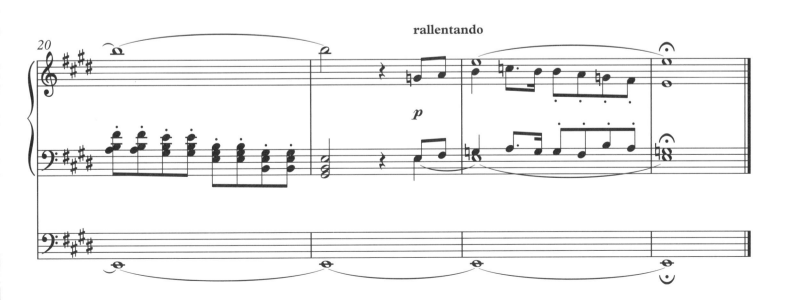

Adoration

FLORENCE BEATRICE PRICE
(1887–1953)

Sw.: Horn 8'
Gt.: Dulciana 8'
Ped.: Gedackt 16'

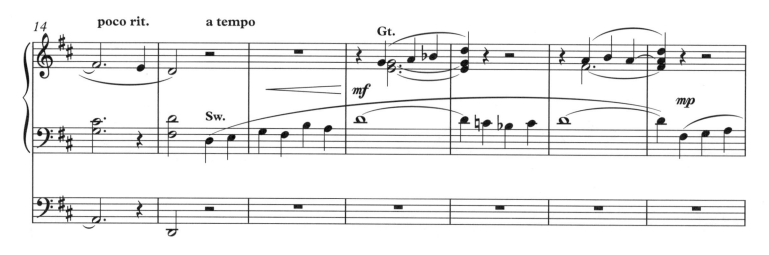

Chorale Prelude on
'Wachet auf, ruft uns die Stimme'

('Wake, O wake! with tidings thrilling')

MAX REGER
(1873–1916)

un poco rit.

Chorale Prelude on
'Wie schön leuchtet der Morgenstern'

('How brightly shines the Morning Star')

MAX REGER
(1873–1916)

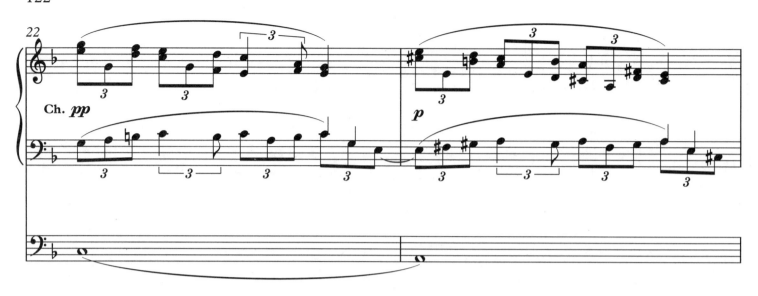

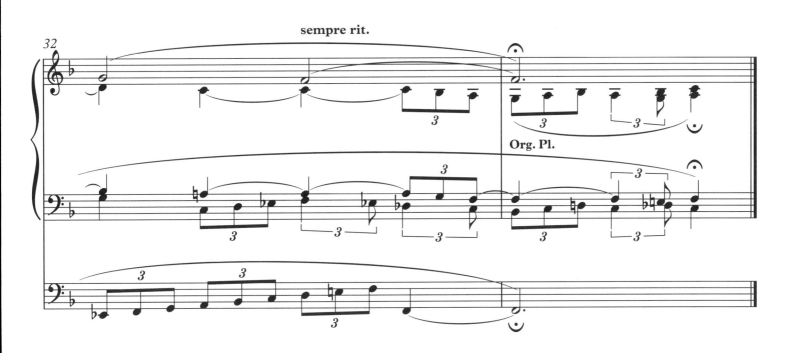

Pastorale

from *Oratorio de Noël*, Op. 12

CAMILLE SAINT-SAËNS
(1835–1921)
arr. Martin Setchell

Christmas Bells

HOWARD SKEMPTON
(b. 1947)

Composer's note: the tempo is moderate, allowing for the possibility of subtle (perhaps involuntary) rubato—too subtle to specify. If it seems natural to relax the tempo a smidgen at the close, I'm happy about it. It would be wilful not to allow it, and no less wilful to require it.

Prelude on 'Deck the Halls'

AMY SUMMERS
(b. 1996)

Chant de Noël

JOHANN PACHELBEL
(1653–1706)
arr. Alexandre Guilmant
and Robert Gower

Réc.: Hautbois. (Boîte ouverte.)
Pos.: Salicional 8', Flûte douce 4', Nasard 2⅔'
ou G.O.: Flûte harmonique 8'
Péd.: Soubasse 16', Bourdon et Violoncelle ou Flûte 8'

Based on the German chorale 'Vom Himmel hoch, da komm ich her' ('From heaven above to earth I come').